Selected and Last Poems

Books by Paul Zweig

Poetry
Against Emptiness
The Dark Side of the Earth
Eternity's Woods
Selected and Last Poems

Prose and Criticism
The Heresy of Self Love
Lautréamont: The Violent Narcissus
The Adventurer
Walt Whitman: The Making of the Poet

Autobiography
Three Journeys: An Automythology
Departures

Selected and Last Poems
Paul Zweig

Edited and with an Introduction by
C. K. Williams

 Wesleyan University Press
Middletown, Connecticut

All inquiries and permissions requests should be addressed to the
Publisher, Wesleyan University Press, 110 Mt. Vernon Street, Middle-
town, Connecticut 06457

Library of Congress Cataloging-in-Publication Data
Zweig, Paul.
  Selected and last poems / Paul Zweig.
    p. cm. — (Wesleyan poetry)
  Introduced by C. K. Williams.
  ISBN 0-8195-2158-2 ISBN 0-8195-1159-5 (pbk.)
  I. Williams, C. K. (Charles Kenneth), 1936– . II. Title.
III. Series.
PS3576.W4A6 1989
811'.54—dc19   89-5417
                                              CIP

Manufactured in the United States of America

FIRST EDITION

Wesleyan Poetry

Contents

Introduction by C. K. Williams   vii

From *Against Emptiness*

On Discovering a Thighbone under a Heap of Stones   3
Walking over Brooklyn   4
God's Ledger   5
A Sadness from the Old Philosophers   6
On Possessions   7
Afraid That I Am Not a Poet   8
The Natural History of Death   9
America at War   12
Pastoral Letter   13
Against Emptiness   14
Self and Soul   15
The Bicycle Odyssey   17

From *The Dark Side of the Earth*

Getting Older   23
The Dark Side of the Earth   24
Losing a Friend   25
The Archaeology   26
Amanita Phalloidus   28
Robinson Crusoe's Notebooks   29
Listening to Bells   30
The Black Stone   31
The City of Changes   32

From *Eternity's Woods*

Aunt Lil   37
Snow   40
The Esplanade   41
Stanzas in an Emergency   44
Prayer Against Too Much   46
The Perfect Sleepers   47
The River   48

A Fly on the Water   51
Jacob and the Angel   52
A Theory of Needs   53
Hope   54
The Art of Sacrifice   55
One Summer Before Man   56
Anything Long and Thin   58
Breaking   59
Bless the Earth, Bless the Fire   60
This You May Keep   61
Life Story   62
The House   64
The Question   69
Wasps   70
Early Waking   71
Parting the Sea   72
And Yet . . .   73
The Other Ocean   74
The Taking Away   75
Eternity's Woods   76
The End Circulates in the Wide Space of Summer   78

Last Poems

Space Is the Wake of Time   81
The Correspondence   82
Piero   83
Skywriting   85
The Thick World   86
Poem: Why can't anything stay still?   88
Poem: The farmers are pumping water from the river   89
Poem: I don't know if I can bear this suddenly   91
Poem: To know it all deeply, to know every detail   93

Introduction

"Afraid that I am not a poet," Paul Zweig begins a poem in his first book, *Against Emptiness*. For some poets, the act of writing a poem is not the simple singing out of the overflowing soul common wisdom reports to us, so much as it is a test of character. The tensions implied in this trial have nothing to do with timidity, faintheartedness, or any of the many neuroses that can inflict the writer. They have instead to do with the poet's conception of the poem, with what the poem asks, with what he or she believes it is capable of. Whether consciously or unconsciously, the poet commits to a kind of gamble that is based primarily in a largeness of ambition, in nearly impossible longings both for the poem and for the self. The poem demands more than verbal felicity, more than musical ingenuity, more than imagistic or metaphoric agility, because what the poet has in mind for it are matters of the spirit, questions of ultimate identity, of transcendence and exaltation. The self which might create such a poem is a creation, too, one which will make unusual and exacting demands.

Of all the intricate questions, literary, aesthetic, historical, and moral, which must be confronted before a poet can write a poem, the most subtle and the most difficult have to do with issues of spiritual identity. For the poet, as for anyone else, the great questions of existence have to do with the tensions between what there is in our characters to which we must resign ourselves and what we believe is perfectible, which requires our best energies for its sometimes very problematical realization. In the poet, though, this struggle is intensified, because what the poet is trying to discover about the self, about strength and weakness of character, about the possibilities of the soul and about its limits is both the subject of the work and its medium. For the poet whose ambitions reach beyond the desire simply to generate verse, whose wishes for the self may not be congruent with general human aspirations but are focused instead on the difficult attempt at informing the ordinary with the transcendent, there are terrific risks. The subjects of poems, the themes of poems, are always in the process of moving beyond themselves: a poem of love can also be a poem of lust for mystical union, an homage to a family member can become an expression of the sad dissatisfactions the poet senses in ordinary perception and ordinary community.

Everything can seem to be at risk during the time of the poem: the spiritual condition of the poet, his or her personal past and future, the social and historical situation in which the poem is taking place, and, finally, the very right of the poet to attempt to compose the poem.

"Afraid that I am not a poet," the poem begins, but then goes on, "Yet willing to write / Even about that . . ." thus expressing both the fearfulness involved in Zweig's conception of the poet's task and the courage that will be characteristic of his work throughout his poetic career. From the earliest poems, Zweig was involved with the kind of demanding spiritual conflict we find in the most adventurous literature. "Afraid that I am not a poet . . ." How to even begin, the poem seems to be saying, when there are such territories to be charted, such forbidding realms of self to be meditated? More rendingly, as the poet senses the ultimate dangers of such undertakings, the poem asks, "How can I be sane with borrowed faces?" But the undertaking is irrevocable now, the poetry is underway, the process, which will absorb the rest of Zweig's creative life, is wholly involving.

In Zweig's early poems, the existential obsessions of the work are often expressed in these sorts of direct questions, posed with an almost naïve obsessiveness: "What have you done to need life so badly?" ("The Natural History of Death"); "Where is the terror that rots under the shirt front?" (the same poem); "How can I escape the invisible father and mother?" ("America at War"). At first, the poet doesn't seem quite to understand the real import of his own projects. The questions the poems ask can seem plaintively off the point, as though the poet felt only a generalized unease, a quandary about his purpose. What will later become the precise substance of a desire for transcendence, for the comprehension of a reality beyond the quotidian, here is expressed with only the vaguest sense of the specificity of the poems' real possibilities. Often there is a somewhat nostalgic regret, the traditional romantic glancing back toward the past as though there, perhaps, the unity, the harmonies that existence promises, may already have been experienced, but with a consciousness not yet sufficient to recognize them. Even the most personal, intimate past is called into question, is made a part of the adventure of the poem. History itself becomes a variable in the struggle, as do religious and philosophical investigations and the genealogies of literary and artistic imagination. The poems struggle in their formulations: images occur, portions of reality swim in and out of significance, symbols take on resonance, are noted, but quickly lose their intensity and their efficacy. In the course of a single poem they are elaborated, exhausted, and some-times even become the occasion for irony or self-mockery, because of their false or at least transitory illusoriness. But at the same time there are, always, in the core of the poems, beneath their apparent uncertainties and confusions, the rigorous demands Zweig would always require of himself, and of his work.

Later, in *Eternity's Woods*, the propositions of inquiry become more subtle, more complex, and still more demanding: "To exist at the highest level; / To be entirely conscious, so that even my smallest sigh / Glides happily, and the deathwatch is never bored . . ." ("Stanzas in an Emergency"). The soul longs quite articulately here toward something beyond the din of relationship and of intellectual quest. The soul longs, and attempts, and fails, at least at first. Reality itself begins to be called into question, the very matrix of being, of self, the origins of self and the manifestations of self as they find form in the gentler elements of human possibility: love, companionship, family, the consolations of solitude. The issue is whether the poet will be able to continue to exist in the state of partial realization, partial consciousness, partial being that the poems manifestly are struggling against now. The drama of the poems often becomes entirely philosophical and spiritual. What the consciousness seems to be seeking now is unremitting progress, growth. The growth of the mind itself has risks, though, because as mind becomes more aware of its potentials, of its own awarenesses, and hence of its freedoms and responsibilities, it demands more of itself: there appear more assumptions of attainment, of improve-ment, of the possibilities that soul must entertain and attempt with the larger scope it has been offered. Also, with so much commitment to consciousness, dangers appear. The poems now clearly begin to confront the various inertias the world of reality holds for us, the delusions of attachment: all the genres of spiritual suicide a civilization with no apparent soul offers the besieged self; greed, hubris, intellectual satiety, and the sheer weariness the project of fulfillment entails.

Zweig offered his soul up to these uncertainties in a way that is rare in American poetry. His poetry from the beginning was driven by the questions he asked himself, and sometimes, in the dramatic energy with which he sought to answer them, along with the skepticism so natural to his mind, he almost seemed to become the victim of himself. This theme, in fact, comes up again and again in his poetry: the self riven by the difficult and uncertain needs of self, the self asking the apparently impossible from itself, and even the self that is as fragmentary as these fragmentary acts of imagination, the poems, that somehow spring from it. The poems themselves, these miraculous, but in some ways utterly unforeseeable productions of consciousness, were to be marveled at with gratitude and delight, but also with a sense of distrust. This delight and this distrust make for a dialectic in the very heart of the poems that is fascinating in the confrontations it entails.

In the poems written near the end of Zweig's life, the force of the tireless intellect that drove him to such rigorous questioning, and the generosity, sensitivity, and imaginativeness of his character fused and tempered these struggles. The very last poems, written in a frenzy of inspiration—as the death that he had lived with for six years and that was by now known and not known, dreaded and entirely engrossing, came ever closer—have a spontaneity, a purity, an energy, and a forthrightness that is nearly overwhelming. These astonishing songs, almost without traditional subject matter, are wide-ranging, far-seeing, and resolutely focused. It is as though all of existence itself, life and death themselves, had become certain as the object of the poems' task, and with this certainty of object came certainty of subject. The poet fused absolutely with his poems, becoming as large and high-minded as they were, with a clarity and an assurance of self that was a consummation of all the struggles and all the attempts and false attempts of a life of scrutiny and spiritual adventure.

❧

I have followed the text of the poems that were published in books as they appeared there. The last poems presented problems because they were not quite completed at the time of Paul's death, and were left in very rough form. The versions here are those I compiled for an issue of *The American Poetry Review.* Some punctuation has been altered so as to be consistent with the rest of the book.

C. K. Williams

From *Against Emptiness*

On Discovering a Thighbone under a Heap of Stones

I

I'm waiting for the Druid to claim his bone
In the woodshed. I have dusted and cleaned it,
But the stain of earth remains.
When he comes I will ask him to explain
These ancient stones heaped near the house
Like a ruined altar. Was he the priest
Who swore the earth to silence, or the victim
Whose blood sealed a pact with the spirit
Of revenge? I will ask him why the fields
Roar each night, as if they waited for
An answer; and tell him what cold secrets
I mumble in my fear, when the night air
Echoes them from tree to tree.

II

Spirits of the earth go by, like travelers
Along an empty road. Their bodies shake
Hungrily and their faces stare, but they
Refuse my hospitality. If one of them
Stumbles near me like a scoured bone,
I hold on to him angrily. What news, I ask.
But already my hands close on wet soil.
So it is each time I stop a traveler,
Until I too stumble in the dark field,
A pilgrim now, dying into earth
At every human touch.

Walking over Brooklyn

Black smoke trails from the incinerators,
Bits of cardboard flaming in the cage
On top of tall chimneys.
You are walking over Brooklyn,
Climbing the space between planets.

Below you, the streets have a smell of childhood:
Rows of clotheslines, like an unsteady road
Where only ghosts can walk;
The murderous echo of boys playing
In the damp shadow of tenements.

You can hear them climbing toward you,
Listen! pulling you down
Like a weathered kite, hand over hand.

At the dinner table, old people sit,
Their bodies locked in the shell
Of the long days; in their eyes,
Dim corridors lit by candles,
Like the pure distance I once tasted
In my blood.

God's Ledger

You gave me what I didn't want
And taught me to love it. You fed me
Sweet food, and killed each painful cell
To read the bitter news I stored there:
News of the smile I crammed against my teeth,
Until angels danced on my nerves
And the gates of heaven opened in my eyelids.

I swear to love what you will take away,
I swear that my bones will be a signature
To bind me in all the courts of heaven:

Owed, my body and the death that cures it.
Owed, these torn pockets to collect your charity.
My aim: to lose more than you give,
Lying down in the hole I have made,
Window upon which death leans,
Me.

A Sadness from
the Old Philosophers

I plant my stick in the loose earth,
And now my father lies down beside me.

I mean the old philosophers,
Emerson, Thoreau,
Mirrors broken, put back together
In silence;

And Walt Whitman,
Grazing at the edges of the earth,
Becoming grass.

On Possessions

I
Burning what I own,
Burning this fuel of nerves and money;

Soon I will be a voice hidden among ruins,
Too poor to be flesh.

II
The fire climbs in my lush veins,
Gutting the landscape,
Destroying my fresh gardens
With flowers rejoicing as they burn,
To mourn for me with ashes still warm:
They are new clothing for the skeleton voyager
Who travels where he cannot see,
Letting the emptiness play him like a harp;
His music heard only by the poor
Who play it upon their bones.

III
Did the saints know this, leaping
In the fire, snapping their fingers?
Their bodies hummed quarter tones and half tones;
And the dumbest trooper shrank into his skin,
Knowing that he could reach no further
With his glowing iron; that a god
Smiled in this wound,
And crawled in this burning flesh.

Afraid That I Am Not a Poet

Afraid that I am not a poet,
Yet willing to write
Even about that;
Holding up words I have loved,
Their exploded joys
Have scarred me into life,

And I am frightened suddenly.
For nothing I have been resembles them;
Nothing has stuck to these
Irretrievable bones.

How can I be sane with borrowed faces?
When the fears and pleasures
That tumble my words
Like seasons harvested in love
Are only empty mirrors,
Images floating in a dry sea?

The Natural History of Death

I

I decided at birth to go on living,
Not even my parents convinced me I was wrong.
When the mistake was pointed out
I excused myself,
Alleging my extreme youth.

I liked standing naked in the basement
Shoveling coal into the open furnace.
The heat taught me I had a body
Long before women ever tried.
That is why, even now, love begins for me
In madness, as if this were an answer
To the old question:
What have you done to need life so badly?

II

When they pried open my life
They found
Mechanical toys and a taste for pure light;

They heard a voice calling backward
In the fibers of the body.

I went out late at night, with poems
Rolled under my arm, pasting them
On storefronts and parked cars;
Talking to the desperate faces:
To skeletons softened by light,
And those who were in no hurry to live.

When they pried open my life
They found
A memory twisted as old iron,
Ice-age fingers innocent as murder.

III

Somewhere in my body a cell must still remember
The flower-smells, the carriage floating
Along the paths of the Botanical Gardens
In Brooklyn.

Columns of black smoke slanted over Europe,
Stepladders
For the meek bodies of the burned.

IV

Who felt with me for the delicate bones
Emerging from boyhood?

Still hungry, and with a man's thoughts,
I ransacked the quiet rooms.
Empty, the world was served up to me,
Like derelict children, piling up
Minute by minute.
They stiffened, and I pressed them
In an old book, before they lost their color.

V

Like mirrors, my hands
Held only what was put into them.
Scraps of paper drowned near the curb
In the rushing water, bearing
My possessions, one by one:
My love for words;
Glasses filled with wax, flickering
For the dead,
Praying for me out of my mother's fear,
And her mother's wild thoughts
In Poland,
Dreaming of the Revolution.

VI

Later, guns learned to resist us,
Firing salvos of raw meat;
The sweet smile of men unwilling to live
Set fire to their houses.

We were sleepy old men, coming of age;
Silent men,
Far in advance of the dictionary.

But the quiet people would not grow up;
They practiced making love under their beds,
They practiced living forever.

Where is the terror that rots under the shirt front?
Where is the child who climbed
On the back of a dog, and crossed America? . . .

VII

At thirty, a man discovers that he has told
A secret. His eyes whisper, while the shouting
In his head goes on, too quick to understand.

The wasted minutes hang
Like a halo of lines around his face.

Words become human as they sink out of reach,
Already bored with being said,
But sweaty,
Expectant. His words listen to themselves,
Like an eye gradually closing,
Making the body-ruins transparent,
But who is there to be seen?

America at War

I

I work at night, carried
By conveyor belts from one sex to another,
Tired of being loved.

When I kill, it is complicated,
Instantaneous.
I crouch inside the gun,
Waiting for the detonation, fondling
Letters from home.
In a moment I will spring,
Knowing
That technology cannot replace me.

II

How can I escape the invisible father and mother?
Their obedient anger
Reaping swaths of broken trees
In the green wood?

My longing cannot be silenced,
It quivers in these cold buildings.

III

Even the elephants know us,
As they wallow in gasoline fumes,
Refusing to make love,
The rivers of elephant pleasure
Corked up in their great legs.

Pastoral Letter

I will name nature's poisons.

Chiendent, the spread of its roots
Like a slum of hungry mouths.

Mushroom, nourishing danger,
Sweated by feverish oaks and chestnuts,
Their delectable cancer.

Angular rocks, scales of the great leprosy,
Torn by God's wheel of changes
Working its wound into the earth.

Viper, threading the grass
With its charge of perfect electricity.
Beetles designed by Picasso to be African gods.
Lizards so harmless I lie awake
Imagining their secret weapon.

These are my companions in your green plague,
Virgin of sweet rot. In my anguish
I match you poison for poison, and fight off
Your blandishing quiet. I dine upon
A soup of nerves and bask in the human,
My body bent into a sign against your
Treachery of flowers.

Against Emptiness

I

Whatever surrounds the raw body of wind
And rolls over me in silence;
Whatever I am this screaming silence for . . .

I want to climb to you, foot by foot,
Along the prayer ladder:
Dusky flower,
Gloom tree in the nerves,
And then my body rigged with magic,
Crying to fill that great invention, your emptiness,
Your tricky silences between stars.

II

The prophet casts his life upon the water;
Upon the waking fish and those, asleep,
Who interpret their solitude without end.
They ascend by their teeth,
By the cell rot of unaccomplished days,
Each small death tidied into words, until
The walls of dead enclose them, and they are
Grateful to be remembered by their failures.

III

Know these words: demon, angel,
And they will follow as you climb
From pit to pit, leaving behind each day
A cell of your rage, a life,
Until, exhausted into wisdom,

Your face will ease you into death;
Your wise face, shedding its peacefulness
Like a lie upon your angry children,
Your patient devils, and the intricate
Joy of the angels you never named.

Self and Soul

The dwarf tears at his clothes
To greet the quietness.
He nudges me to show him what I write,
Although he knows all about my longing.
If I'm not careful, he'll
Tear the page and wipe himself with it.

When he falls under a chair, cooing
Like a baby, I will overcome
My native cowardice and trample him.
He will beg me to stop, but I'll
Soak him in whiskey and light a match
To it—by the flickering glare
Lying down with a book, to read:
Poetry, I think, about quietness
And corn growing, waking up somewhere
Too happy to wake up.

❧

I have made my peace with the monster.
I will give him what I have,
In return he will give me nothing,
But I don't complain, for he
Is nervous and will drink himself mad
Before long.

Each night I dream of killing him,
But he knows the art of guilt.
He sleeps when I sleep, when
I eat, the food enters his mouth.
Making love, he lies down for me,

And he knows my ignorance:
The fear that when he lives for me,
I have no life: it is the fear
Eating and waking up, the noise
Of the body taking my place.

᪇

Tired now, he has fallen asleep.
And I remember what it is like
To have lost the power of movement;
To live only vertically;
To become a tree.

The Bicycle Odyssey

I

Sleep is no death, no familiar ordeal.
I will get up now and shape my body hopefully;
I will barricade this wild skin that brings its messages
To me past sleeping lions and monkeys,
And a chandelier of bones that sheds its light
Inside my body.

I will leave the small, mobile prisons:
My home where the space under the walls
Has been hollowed out by fear;
Streets rubbed smooth by the moon,
Like pale sandpaper humming over the curb
And the parked cars, and the stiff sex of the streetlights.

II

My wife looks out at me from the parked cars
And bangs at the windshield; she turns on
The radio, listening for news of the spirit.
There is my father, squatting on a leaf
High over the sidewalk. He follows the gentle
Footprints of a searchlight across the stars.
It is looking for a thin crack in the sky,
Leading to a place inside his thoughts
Which he has never loved.

He sits in the highest branches of the tree
As if he were enclosed in his name,
Waiting for me to wake up and return him to his body.

III

But I leaped on my old bicycle and hurried to the beach.
Sleep is a diving bell, a portable adventure.
The water curled aside and lisped.
It spread rugs of seaweed over my sleeping madness
And down I went, pedaling on the back of an eel.
As I went, my shirt fell off, and my pants;
Last of all I lost my straw hat.

IV

At the bottom of the sea I found a wrecked ship,
Its ribs twisted out of shape,
Its crew lifting and falling with the current
Like a field of lilies
Waiting to be resurrected. Strangest of all
Were its green sails that strained with the tide,
Glowing and stiff, a clear foliage of canvas.
I recognized the crew and called them by their names.
"Flowerpod," I called, "Skycraper, Naked Bottle!"
"Words, words," they gurgled back at me,
"They sink in water and don't taste very good."

V

And then the lilies began to sing:

> A stovepipe hat
> and a motor car
> flew round and round
> the morning star.
>
> A flatiron
> Straightened out the sky,
> until the star
> began to cry.
>
> Then something
> in a trolley car
> tugged the sky
> around the star.
>
> Round and round
> the star they went,
> until the very sky
> was bent.
>
> Sink the sea
> and go to shore;
> your love don't love you
> anymore.

Their singing swam around me. It nibbled at my chest
And plucked my hair, and almost woke me up;
Until I rode away and put my sleep to sleep.

VI

I was naked, for my mind had fallen open.
But the lilies bowed and scraped;
They waved their boneless arms and saw,
As in an old movie, the bicycle,
The skinny legs, the awkward greeting
Of this man who had not known them.

VII

I saw an old man
With strands of seaweed between his legs,
Bright fish where his eyes had been.
He counted the days on a rosary of glowing stones.
Now and then he picked a day from the string,
Rough, angular, fiery, and ate it;
Tears rolled from his cheeks onto the ocean floor,
Where they lay, hardened by salt and cold,
Until this man, this father of all days,
Slipped one hand,
Beaked and marvelous like a cuttlefish,
Onto the pile of the days.

VIII

Then my bicycle rusted and I had to swim.
My skin fell off and I had to walk.
My legs melted and stretched,
My eyes wandered on a green thread
That I could lengthen or pull in, like radar.

I saw a woman buried in the sand;
She wore the ocean like a body.
Mother! I cried, crawling with eight strong arms
Over the sand.

IX

The wild, thinking water I had become
Arranged itself in ranks,
A transparent army, rushing through the fields
Of water, undiluted, tickled by long
Fingers of the moon.

Striped, spiney fish played inside me.
Electric eels plugged into me,
Sputtering messages. The whole ocean
Was resurrected by the currents
Of my intelligent, salty body.

From *The Dark Side of the Earth*

Getting Older

Advancing into sleepless woods,
Each year the ice getting thinner,
And the trapped waters darker;
The mind's frosty ballet superbly staged
On a floor of nerves;
Breath shorter, skin veined and rough;
Understanding a woman's precarious beauty
For the first time,
I stand in a frozen year,
And hear the whisper of darkened lives.
Do the words come from inside or out?
That sort of knowledge eludes me now.

Sometimes, when I go for a walk,
I see an old man's face smiling without humor.
His fleshy lips resemble an ear
Moving cautiously without any sound.
He waits for me at the end of a milky street
Which turns unpredictably into swamp or rust.
It is the old man I may never reach,
Distracted by everything that must be lived,
My hands twitching like butterflies in the brief sunlight.

The Dark Side of the Earth

December 1972

We don't talk about the war anymore,
Living on the dark side of the earth,
The winter side,
Yet we do not keep silent either.
We repeat ourselves until the words
Become thin as insect husks,
Forgetting the stripped faces, the soup of limbs
Left when bombs have fallen.
It is dark here, a peculiar winter.
The ice storm caught us unawares
And we froze into busy postures and went on living,
But the inmost room in our bodies was a grave.
How else could bombers inch across the sunlight,
And the earth get drunk with shudders,
And the dead be indistinguishable from mud,
If our most comfortable nightmares
And our innocent wealth did not belong to death?
When words make nothing happen they turn against the sayer.
We are eaten by our words, and so are silent,
And don't talk about the war anymore.

Losing a Friend

When the anger finally came
We were startled to find how much we already knew
About dead friendships,
Breaking the words off, shoving the ends
Into each other's faces.
During those long walks along the Drive
We argued about men whose guts were clothed in talk,
Not knowing we were talking about ourselves.

Had warfare always existed in your muscular face?
Had my anger spurted for years
From deeps I never knew,
Silted over in the furthest bottom of myself?

I can smell the charred earth, windows
Gaping like broken mouths,
And the killing that goes on because a man
Keeps to what he knows best. Meeting on the street,
We will nod and say a few words, or pass and say nothing.
Yet we remain strangely intact in each other's minds
Like bodies buried yards deep in stone,
Without warmth or change,
Until our shadows stretch thin as drums,
And the time wearies of itself.

The Archaeology

I

My first God was a tenement:
Warty red bricks, a net of cast iron
Slanting down a wall.
It looms in the before-dawn sweat,
Offered through the window as a covenant
That we survive each night;
That days float out of the stale darkness,
Busy with miracles.

II

We are married to each other's nights;
The sky a gray slice over a brush of trees.
It is Parmenides' world, the temptation of stone,
Where all lives are the same.
A dog whimpering is a heart, a butcher's rack is a hug,
A blind man is a mirror, a pistol is a gulp of blue wine.

III

My anxious lies will be discovered by archaeologists
In the tenth layer, under burnt ships
And the broken bones of horses.
They will have the apologetic look of hearthstones,
Singed by the ordinary sadness of living.

That was before the virus of heroes had ruined our minds.
I grew up with no biography
As stones grow up, or the weather.
It was like fishing without a hook.

In the city of the tenth layer
The son had not ripped fire from his father's loins,
Wisdom was not a virgin born out of an ear,
The soldier did not stink from secret wounds,
The poet had not invented silence,
His wife had not yet learned to love death.

When the diggers came, they found burnt pots,
But the shadows had fled.
Instead of songs, a coprolith;
Instead of heaven, scratch marks on a wall,
The relic of bad dreams.

IV

I want to gnaw at my jailer's shadow.
I want to write to my brothers in crime
Whose victims get rich,
While they squat in stale rooms
Rolling snake-eyes with their heart-bones.
I want to sing of claustrophobia,
The iron marriage of a man to his shadow.

Hugging the sprawled sheets, the grease,
And the insomnia;
Inspecting the entrails of birds;
Speaking ghost-talk to my wife
Although my anxiety shines through her
Without casting a shadow;

I will praise the fear of death
Which is the basalt of dark foundations;
I will trace a map for caravans setting out
Tomorrow across the blinding floor.
I will tell my secrets, listening in secret
To find them out.

V

I did not write these words; I scraped them into stone
Like a prisoner loosening the bars with his bare hands.
My poem is an empty window, and a leap to freedom:
Softly blinking leaves, the horizon
Cupped suddenly under the sky.
It is a long fall as birds do it,
Shorter this way.

Amanita Phalloidus

To be alone in the woods, poking at the moist odors
For mushrooms, knowing the diffuse sexuality
Which comes after a long rain has soaked the forest floor,
And the sun has begun its languorous tattoo
Past the chestnut leaves, and the dark pointed branches.

Around me lie the dusky skins of mushrooms.
I love these shade-gnomes
Meditating in the brown whisper of leaves.
They spring up and melt away in days,
Leaving behind a meaty smell which the wind dissolves.
After each rain they glide back again, standing idly
In the mottled quiet, like Homer's ghosts
Staring at travelers in the underworld.

Here is one I recognize.
I get down on my knees, and scrape away
The furry twigs around its base,
Its green head shaking imperceptibly.
Amanita phalloidus:
Sexual head poking from the moist loam at my feet.
In these gnarled woods, the old confusions return.
The earth's erection is a mother phallus,
A pale eye nodding in the temple of my knees.
Leaning over, I see its speckled skin,
Its fish-white spores,
Its milky egg sifted over with soil

I know that one bite would be suicide,
Like a pause in the wind, when the fainter hum
Of insects can be heard. I am not tempted,
Yet I find it hard to look away,
As if I were kneeling over a well
Whose moist echoes urged me to lean over more,
Still more, until my arms lurched forward,
And I fell into the perfect night of the earth.

Robinson Crusoe's Notebooks

When I am alone,
The world becomes an erotic dream.
Sex boils in my shoes,
I plunge my penis into every open flower.
Bushes sway, pendulous and ripe;
I touch them timidly.
On my hilltop of erect green leaves
The other words are gone:
Friends, lovers, acquaintances;
The quiet surrounds them like a moist palm.

My skin explores the earth.
Pine shadows touch me, and I yield,
Wading in their milky darkness,
Afraid to have a name,
Afraid it will search me out
Like a shirt of weariness.

Silence is sex,
Solitude is sex.
The unused body blossoms into sex.
Earth color of marmalade,
Failed wells inside me spitting dust
And broken stones,
Suddenly you are filled with water,
Like a hand kneading my soft flesh,
Drooped over me by the slow wind of sex,
And the warm wind of sex . . .

Listening to Bells

I hear bells ringing in the village,
Filling the valley with their deep liquid sound.
They mean that someone has died today,
Maybe the old woman on the hilltop facing mine.
She dressed in black for so many years,
Death was paid for on arrival; it came like the lover
She took half a century ago, when vineyards
Grew where the woods are whispering with bells.

Sometimes I've tried to visit the church
On a ruined back street of the town.
It's always locked, except for pigeons nesting
Under the eaves, and for the dead
Who have the key. They pull the bell rope
Hanging down beside the altar,
Pumping the sound of death out into sunlight.

Bells ring over the oaks and the walnuts;
Over this house cast away in grass, acacia thorns,
And those dark thorns turned inward
Like a dream of terror.

The valley hums with the news death flings
Over its woods and fields, over its heaps
Of damp stone left by the Druids,
Remembered now only by wasps and spiders,
But touched, almost trembling, by the bells
Rolling past, even when the church
Has been locked again, and strands of rope
Touch the floor in one moist heap,
And there is no sound I can hear
Except my life whispering, bell-like,
In the patient morning.

The Black Stone

I
Death was my first appetite,
I've had others since.

Black stone I swallowed on the day I was born,
You are the loneliness fattening in my breath;
You cross out each word I stumble toward,
Saying help.

On mornings of smooth stone,
And mornings of grass curled, pale and dreamy,
Underneath the stone,
I know you are a nugget of black ice
Working your way down inside me.

II
You are closer to me than flesh,
You are the knot of loose ends I breathe;
A tear wept
In the closed weather of the stone.

Sometimes when I'm bored or sleepy
I can feel you under my eyelids,
Incredibly patient;
You take a lifetime to go from here to there.

The City of Changes

Venice 1973

I

Returning to thunder, white buildings,
And a damp smell rising from the sidewalk.
Lightning plunges through me, exposing
The gray wall I lean against
Like Rodin's half-carved statues.

I feel sympathy for the motionless water,
It is a mirror with no gift for images,
A cat's eye attuned to the miracle of loneliness,
Maneuvering in the shadowy space with sure feet.

Remembering too much or too little,
I have the solidity of a rainstorm,
Beating sudden fingers into oily water,
Molding myself minute by minute
To this beautiful grave.

II

What comes from water must return to it;
First the image goes, later we follow.

This passage over black sand,
This passage between names we know as thirst;
Searching for shadows where the light fails and we begin,
Bearing maps, compass, legible stars,
And a sound rising in concert that does not touch the silence,
Merging, cell by cell, into one bodily song.

Listen!
It is the city subsiding into patience
Under rose-colored bricks;
It is the green anguish of doorsills;
It is the tide feeling its way along marble steps;
It is a floor for echoes;
It is the impossibility of touching what we see,
Carried further by death, so much further.

III
These are the changes we know:
A desert whispering into flower,
A lover betrayed,
A tree choosing its darkness.

Each day we fail, sitting in forgotten chairs,
Changing our sex, our color,
Loving what we hate.
We choose our death over again.
Like a bride without smiles
We marry the stone husband who hugs us,
Our perfect shadow, inscribed with our name.

My exhausted eyes, my face
Staring up at me from the water,
Are traveler's wounds.
Beneath them hides the life the wild man saw
Like a sediment in his cup of visions.

IV
Adrift on the surface of death,
He caressed its images, and they spoke to him,
Stirred by a strange wind which crept out of roots,
Rasping and sighing, for they spoke with his own breath:

"Come into the marketplace,
Come into the city of changes
Where we live, as in a mirror.
Having given up your name, you will move
Across the space of death without hindrance.
You will be a link between all things,
A road of images.

"The heavy flesh of dahlias,
Their translucid green stems,
Whatever smolders in its own sunlight,
—Bird, fish or man—barters its name
And its memory in the marketplace of death.

"You will be the bridge and the water under it.
You will be the soil and the root.
You will be the blood and the vein it flows through.
You will be the rock and the wind.
The poem plunges in your flesh,
Its needle wounds you. You are its food.
Only in you can the poem become alive."

   V
We are a soil for violent flowers.
We eat envy, anguish is our poem.
Yet things become beautiful in our company.

This day is cool and bright.
Behind each gate geraniums burst like glances,
The ocean extends its patient fingers between the buildings.
The peace we cannot live surrounds us,
Penetrating the pores of buildings.

It is our gift to another century,
Like the unburied ghosts of heroes
Who walk at night and leave their messages.
Things grow old in it and become human,
As we cannot do.

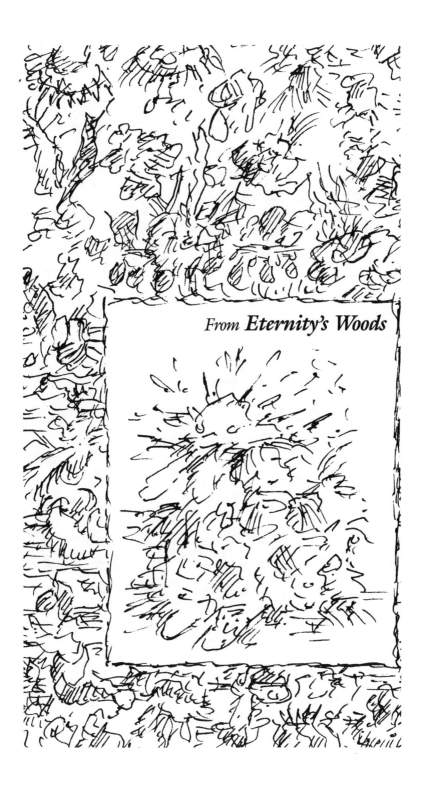

From **Eternity's Woods**

Aunt Lil

I

They brought her to the hospital
On one of those April days
That remind us we will never live enough.
That the soft smell of leaves, flowering breeze,
The silver light flashing from windows,
Will always be too much for us.

She kicks the covers back, not caring
If we see her enormous thighs, her birthmark
Tufted with secret hairs only lovers had seen.
When her lips won't form around her thought,
She cries out girlishly, "I don't know, I don't know."
Her large eyes roll and stare, as if looking
For someone to pry her from her failing flesh.

II

A beach: scalloped sand, soft rasping waves;
My parents searching frantically to see
If I had drowned, or if, like the fish
In the tale, I could breathe their angry
Guilt and make a life of it.
With a small boy's genius, I imitated childhood,
Taking you, my large-eyed beautiful aunt,
To love passionately and simply.

Cruel and soaring,
You battered those you loved,
As if ecstasy and cruelty were the same.
Yet at times you were happier than anyone;
So drunk on yourself, you could hardly
Walk down stairs for the stumbling heavens at your heels.

III

I remember sitting with you on the subway,
Thick-headed with fever.
You opened your newspaper
To a cloud boiling on a stalk of light,

A single word, Hiroshima.
Amid the screeching of subway metal,
The headlines drooping on front pages, your voice,
Your immense body, seemed to fill the subway car.

I hadn't heard yet of your manic flights,
The electroshock, the family's
Embarrassed hush at your desperate ways.

You were sick of too much:
Hope fucking laughter.
Yet to me you were beautiful,
A brown moon of flesh.
And the boy who lived as in a cold sleep
Came strangely forth into your larger louder life.

IV
Old death,
Will you come with me today
To meet someone I love?
We can walk there along the river
Past tenements of red brick,
And barely thickening April branches:
The river's grey-shine spinning past us,
An orange tugboat,
A low-swimming freighter out toward Jersey.

Will you teach me about her rooms
Filled with a westward light,
Her books thumbed and bright along one wall?
Nowhere the smallest hint of a failed life,
No dust balls of loneliness or fright.

Yesterday I sat on her bed,
Holding her soft old woman's hands.
She forgave me for being young,
For the scared distance I put between us all these years.
Her enormous eyes never looked at me,
Only her hands spoke,
Her fingers stirring so I would know.

Old death,
The more I see you, the more
I know of restless eyes, vulnerable mouths,
Uncertain language of lips.

For I have learned what I came for:
My mad old aunt loved life.
She only hurt us when she was afraid
That it would burst in her.
She never gave in to her old age,
But expelled it from her,
And hung clean sweet living upon her walls.

Snow

Love is all we could manage,
Its particles floating from the hard rim of the air.
Our tracks were clear in the fresh chance
Heaven threw behind us. The pain
Went on searching behind your face,
The snow went on falling.

Once your voice worked so gently into my brain,
It took root in the mind-dark
And branched forth again, singing.

Character may be a failure of love;
This morning, I want to love you,
And the birch trunks invisible on snow,
Your hand pushed warmly into my pocket;
I want to love the darkening blue at the sky's edge,
Our thoughts fumbling to hold on;
I want to love our breath-smoke warming
The air, then vanishing
In the frozen February day.

The Esplanade

I

The ocean churns onto the old slabs
And old iron, as my father and I clamber
Over the esplanade in our jogging sneakers.
A hurricane shattered it when I was a boy,
But now the broken slabs, the color of bread,
And the prongs of wrenched iron, like crawlers
Weeping rust onto the eroded pavement,
Are a zone of permanent ruin along the water's edge.
Weeds thrust from cracks and scratch our legs.
My father's almost eighty years
Have cured him to lean, silent stiffness.

For years he worked nights, and slept all day
In a stale room at the other end of the house,
His head wedged under the pillows.

I imagine him clutching some gift
Along the tenement streets, when he was a boy,
Working at his father's laundry.
He preserved it in his mind,
A timeless falling world where he still lives;
The gift was for me:
An amazed distance only acrobats could leap.

II

I spent summers here as a boy,
Peering out at the Rockaways,
At the white scooting chips of sailboats.
The bay was windswept, sparkling;
Its emptiness was half inside me.
I lay on a tilted slab, a radio jammed by my ear,
Listening to the love songs of those years:
Heartaches and night sweats were my music then,
As if my mind were a shell where something
Had drunk deep. It was the first of many rooms,
A blur of enclosure: a bedroom rank with adolescent sex,

Another room over Paris rooftops,
A bronze lamp, a clock with a twisted hour hand;
The innocuous matter of days
That took an impression, like soft wax.

This morning we follow the esplanade,
Full of awkward silence, athletic, lean,
Already preparing to jog into the next world.
My father talks in prepared sentences,
Always rehearsing about these waters he has walked
Along every morning for fifty years.
In his constricted voice, almost inaudible,
An exhalation from some crevice in his mind,
He talks about the devil, God's partner
In the human heart. These waves, he says,
May be heaven's heartbeat, but the blood
In our veins is the devil's work.
I too know the devil's work, which brings
Us together here, partners in movement, in failure,
As if he carried me even now in his lean body,
His mind grown sleepy from peering into a dimness.

III
At the far end of the jumbled rock
And cement walk is a chain fence
And a bleak lawn, some unused benches;
The sort of building everyone knows,
A bland skin of squares and angles,
A nest of antennae, empty repeating windows.
As we skirt the fence, my father
Stares at the wintry expanse
Of ocean, grass, the building of tan brick,
With its small orderly windows.
It is a nursing home; my father is an old man.

Sea gulls waddle on the breakwater
Stabbing at bread rinds, or lift off
With powerful thrusts, to skim the incoming waves.
It is a bitter gift: that crashing line of white water,
The meeting of two realms.

My father and I share it now,
Both of us peer into the dimness.
All my life, I have wanted to come closer
To this mild, unforgiving man,
Who exists in my hands and voice,
And is the nervous laughter I hear
Before my throat expels it.

IV

I remember my grandfather's quavering voice,
Sitting beside a window, a few days before he died.
He chanted in Yiddish to his grandson,
Who understood nothing, but stored everything in his memory,
Distended by unsayable fatigue.

An unpainted house, wind singing in the cracks,
The window casting a sheen on the long unused sofa,
The bed with its sad quilt. On the table,
The photograph of a boy with large ears,
A crushed smile, standing beside his father,
Who squints beyond the camera,
A stiff, muscular, beautiful man.

V

Father, there's so much I never asked you,
Now the answers seem trivial.
Yet, for all your angry quiet, your shy nervous body,
What have you saved by living less?

I think of your swallowed angers,
The hurt on your face when I twisted grammar.
All your life, you have wrestled with fears
That would not become angels.
Your crabbed masculinity concealed a motherly
Sweetness you could let out only when you were alone,
With the damp sand at your feet, the foaming waves
Beside you. With an artistry I still marvel at,
You remade yourself in that lonely space,
As you have remade yourself in me.

Stanzas in an Emergency

I

Here is the river,
The salt-tide edging upstream,
Grey cliffs extending in the sunmist.

I will not count my blessings.
I will be blessed.
I will solve the baffled distance in my mind.
I will not panic at my freedom.
I will know the smooth night
When my wife perches beside me,
Plumed and shining, as on a branch.
I will bring the estuary of the grey day
Into everything cramped and scarred.
I will bring you, my puzzled patient friend,
Whom I keep eluding
When you want only to tell me about love.

II

My neighbor emerges
In a clang of tumblers and doors.
With her sad nipples, her daughter vanished into permanent winter,
She is stubborn as a nun, and almost beautiful.
I see the news seller on the corner,
His blind face, his daylong
Conversation with dimes and quarters.
I accept my wife's rage, her pride,
The spined flower standing for her in my mind,
The frantic light which is love's exit, or entrance.

III

To exist at the highest level;
To be entirely conscious, so that even my smallest sigh
Glides happily, and the deathwatch is never bored,
For the little one, God's human face,
Death, with his gay elfin whisper,
All the goings-on in closets,
Smothered giggle, lank defeated clothes;
All, all come crowding in, like guests at a wedding,
With promises that only death can keep.

IV

A stubble-faced Greek runs the all-night
Market around the corner.
His bins are full of mangoes, plums,
Crushed sprigs of mint,
Bananas large as clubs, roots for alien stews.
They are colors that play against the night,
Bins of the loveliness that never sleeps.

This Greek in his shop
Stands guard for me, I sleep for him.
Together we endure the night.

Prayer Against Too Much

Late-summer trees;
White flowers thickening around each house,
Where people eat, touch, talk,
Not disturbing the peace they cast
Over the inward and the outward sleep.

An enormous wish:
That nothing be too plentiful;
That grass diminish into lawns,
And the hunt become a ceremony of love.
This harmony is a prayer against too much.

Behind leaf-shadowed windows,
We peer into one well, waiting
For the soft splashing of a stone
Neither of us throws.
At chance points we touch, create shade, drop leaves.
Gradually we have become each other's weather,
As Ovid knew, glimpsing
The soul's destructive music in a face.

The Perfect Sleepers

This light flooding my chair
Is too strong at six in the morning;
It was meant for the policemen prowling
In a room around some criminal,
His guilt a form of sleeplessness.

With half-shut eyes, I see horses motionless in a field
Except for their tails that flick away darkness,
Their eyes blazing like angels
On a beach in hell, bruised but noble,
For they left speech behind them
On their nightlong fall into the world.

Perfect sleepers, erect in the narrow field
Between thinking and dreaming,
Your large eyes merciful, but empty;
I take you with me into the grey milk of dawn,
Knowing your terrors are simpler than mine:
Afraid of puddles, rabbits and the whip,
Not of promises kept or broken, not of breathing,
Not of love's forged signature
And its costly repairs.

The River

I

A bridge over the low-flowing river;
Houses like torn white cards cling to the cliffside.
Ballfields in the park resemble sexual flowers,
The bruised earth of the pitcher's mound,
Foul lines plunging toward the water.

An all-day news broadcast fills my living room,
And the half-life within: enigmas, voices.

For three years, living over this trough
In the earth, I have watched the slow turning
Of the light; years which wrote their scorchings
And frights on me. In its furrow of rock,
Twenty-four stories down, the river was another world,
Vast, clear and sweet, like a bow
Drawn slowly in one never-wavering note.

When my daughter was an hour old, flailing
In the aseptic glow of the hospital cradle,
Her eyes squeezed shut, already bruised by light,
She made thin, rasping sounds,
As if some creature were trapped behind her gums.

Genevieve, one day
You will remember someone: a glimpse,
A voice, telling you what I never told
—What the living never say—
Because the words ran backward in my breath.

II

The other day, with my daughter at the zoo,
The wild stench of the animal house,
Its cackling and screeching, frightened her.
In one cage, a lynx swung back and forth,
Its eyes half closed, feet soundless as a dancer's.

In our century, imprisonment is our romance.
A man looks out his window
With a somber faith resembling hope:
Out there, the forbidden world of sunlight,
The river and the distant hills, hazy and blue,
Like a glimpse of paradise.

My daughter comes halfway up my thigh,
A thin, serious little girl, but already
She has her secrets. Because her face has no past,
She is still only partly human.
Careless and half-bored, she watches the lynx,
And the two of them, blank, curiously elusive,
Make the sidestep that lets time hurtle by.

III

On summer afternoons, the river ignites
With a soft simmering heat,
Dissolving the space of my room,
As if the earth wheeled its smoky globe before my eyes.

Genevieve, can you hear it?
A bird's hoot, or the wheezing throb of a tug?
Nothing is lost; every memory,
The infinite sensations of every day,
Rise up and cover us.

Here is the river. Its honeyed crawl
From nowhere to nowhere, its gun-metal flow,
Will blink as if it had never been.
And the tugboat pushing barges upstream,
The current crumpling at its prow;
Boys in the park playing baseball
On the brown vulva of the ballfield:
That simplicity is not for us, but we love it.

IV

Walking next to me, your hand wrapped
Around my thumb, your capering body
Seems not to touch the ground.

Octagonal paving stones; a fine spray
Of shadows across the Drive;
The iron skeleton of a Junglegym
Where children clamber and slide.
A block down, drummers thump arpeggios
Hollow notes. Beer cans, paper bags.
The dour gait of joggers,
As if life were always uphill, always older.

The river gleams beyond the stone parapet;
It is a nether sky,
A tail drooped indolently in the sun;
A root branching into a continent.

A Fly on the Water

I

It is eating me.
It is everything hungry in the world,
And wants me, and I'll tell you, I don't mind.
The women I meet are soft fire;
At night,
Space rattles in my heart;
Your voice,
That muffled angry breathing.

My fathers shuffle the sky; odor of pine trees,
Dark sandy soil. I am lonely,
And think of those sad mystical men in their dark hats,
Who made God's noise when they prayed,
Made it louder in their goose-down beds,
When they clapped their wives' ears
And heard God's drum measuring their bones.

II

A child opens his arms
In the summer heat. With eyes half closed,
He feels the life spilling inside him.
Small and pale on the grass,
He looks almost cruel, he is so happy.

The tree shakes, and God falls out;
Lifetimes of skin and longing stroll naked in the street.
Because it is all I know, I do this;
My text, a joke of the flesh, like eyesight, hummingbirds,
Anything that soars.

III

Stillness spreads from your face
Like ice knitting on a pond.
When it breaks, will God stream past my ankle
Darkly, or as a pool of deadly light?

A fly skates on nothing, on tension:
On something as abstract as a prayer, or as love.

Jacob and the Angel

Like a dried husk, split into a grin,
I stood on the slope of the hill, and listened to
Something rising over the crippled acacia,
The spiky weeds goats grind with their flat yellow teeth.
I could hear them, grunting, half-asleep,
In the glimmering starlight, so bright it could be an edge
Of the final fire, just starting out there.
Something rose over the land; not only darkness trailing
After the sun like a tail, something from me.

I licked dew from these rocks when the wells failed,
Drank goat's blood, and lay with my tongue
Pressed against my teeth. Thirst made me a man,
If a man is someone who drinks pain, and is still thirsty.

And then I was thrown down, as if crumpled
By the lid of the stars. I saw a tree
Rising to heaven, like a brain of thorns;
A wing darting downward, as if a hole
Had plunged earthward and struck me.
My cracked brain of a human being
Bled into the ground,
Half-crazed because God had chosen me.
Why won't He leave me alone, my mouth
Full of dust, my shoulders scorched and breaking?

So Jacob tried to struggle free
Of God's thought, and God's parched burden.

A Theory of Needs

I want what has been sliding
Toward me from the corners of the earth;
What the wind lulls along the early morning streets:
The dancing fit of history,
The fathers, my magnificent liars,
Who tugged until the garment tore,
And the tumbling fall began.

Lovers reaching as I go past,
I am thumb-worn as an old table,
A house askew,
The hole in time made by an old photograph.

All right I'll say it! I betrayed, slept, woke up;
Married, died, exulted.
The bird of sympathy howled in my sleep.

I want to jostle strangers in the street,
No knowing which of them stole death.
Poets made it, philosophers disguised it;
It is mine, a bargain.

Hope

A stalk of yellow weed isolated in sunlight;
The tinge eastward toward Queens over tarred rooftops.

A wake furls slantwise across the empty river,
Cloud-shadows slide over the city.
It is slough time,
Night flows from each little death
Hiding under bright covers, rises, fills all of space.

A room lights up across the street,
And the dusty pane gives the awkward man
Shuffling inside it a softness,
As he walks to the window, walks back,
In the wakefulness of his white room,
Its ruffled paper globe over the light bulb,
Alive in no one's eyes.

It comes, you are moving toward it,
You will be alive until you die.
The sadness in people's faces won't be for you.
It will be like weather,
A tattoo of light through gaps in the clouds,
The juttings of light, the splinterings, the wonderings.

The children cough in their sleep,
An indigo sky looms over black walls.
Drip, drip goes the gathered knob of night.
You are contained in your portion of endlessness,
Pregnant as white porcelain.
Catch me, you say, oh, catch me!

The Art of Sacrifice

Our breath on the altar is offered in love.
The fuck-you we smile is offered in love.

The faucet bubbling with anxiety
And the mirror fishing for loneliness,

The worm we cut into lengths and serve,
Calling it day by day, are offered in love.

So much love, and I am hiding,
Exploring inside the wall, pretending no one is there.

One Summer Before Man

Listen! The undergarments of the women
Are rustling OM. It is the Sanskrit
Of skin, the Hebrew of hair.
I have made a breath-tunnel in the air,
And now I plant my kiss upon you,
Naked as a woman in the blue neon of love,
Or as the looping antennae strung over
Miles of the desert in Arizona, which listen
To the spaces between stars, and hear heavy breathing;
Or else as the noiseless snipping
Of surgical scissors as they part the living tissue,
Bringing to light that which had been dark.

So much was known that will not be known.
The ways of the animals; some angles
Of sunlight on a blue window;
Or what the cow-mother said at the crossing
Of the paths, one summer before man,
When nothing had received a name,
And silence had not yet acquired
Its present unutterable scandal
(The scandal of crushed almonds, or of ozone;
Or of industrial processes accomplished by no human hand),
Before even beauty and its needlework,
Which is all that we remember.

Gather close, children, I will tell you
About that bellowing on the hill.
It is the cow-mother whose words
We have stolen for our purpose
(Here is the sack where the severed words lay).
She has no tongue, she bleats at the piss-yellow
Moon, a wheezing asthmatic sigh.
And then, swallowing all the summer's wild grass,
The blackberries, the succulent plants
Spreading their labia under the oak trees;
Swallowing the turds of small animals,
And the clattering of the dragonflies,
Those Japanese warriors, she swells, she swells!
And then, oh, children, from her mouth
Which knows no future because it is toothless,
Backward, and tight as a sphincter,
From her musical anus, she sings.

Anything Long and Thin

All traffickings upward out of the earth
Or sideways across it: longitudes,
Desperations; the glue of sentences
(Their meanings bunched and dense,
A glare of light, a space seizing
You with coarse hands).
Anything long and thin, the idea of poverty,
Love wrested into a question mark
Like a man violently breathing out.
And the train trips, the trajectories of airplanes,
A knife slitting the infinite until it touches home,
And the life stumbles on its imaginary
Thread over the abyss. Ship wakes, rivers,
The shy proddings of the grass.
And then, more tender than eyesight:
Eternity mooning in a glass,
Or a flagpole stubbing itself against the sky.
And everything that won't stay still:
Your swinging hair, your voice reminding me
That God is a freeze-frame in my heart,
Or a flickering in my lymph; or maybe
A silence this evening, looking down
At the barges with their white wakes,
The sea gulls wheeling over the water.
Time flattened by a goldbeater's hammer
Becomes space: buds, twigs, shy leaves,
And a fistful of roots, *chiendent*.
They say we are renewed every seven years,
Except for the scars of past weariness
The Hindus call samskaras.
Only they live on, as a net of furrows on our brain,
The small lightnings that dim our eye.

Breaking

Scissors; the farting of outboard
Motors; the muscular stranglings
Of the foul wind that blows from whatever empty well,
From whatever gateway into the garden from the clanging house,
From whatever lung-pit dug into cold hills,
And now emitting breakages and pearls, figurines and turds;
All those remnants, all those shards;
While the unbroken wind coils
Around the earth grasping its tail.
Earthworms part, hardly noticing that they are two.
Seeds break from the mother tree;
Lovers go about with their wounded stumps;
I turn from you and see the incredible chill of space.
Patience! The paramecium will inherit the earth.
A face will pass by in that swarming
Solitude which is the soul's light.

Bless the Earth, Bless the Fire

Here is the wanderer with
His unwrapped soul, his parcels of pure voice.
Oh, cloud of unravelings,
Root hairs of the saints descending
Into the sorcerer's night with obsidian tools
Of silence, to root out the unspoken ones,
Food for the thought which is never thought.

Take a flint egg, hatch it.
Take a mouth that hasn't spoken for a thousand years,
A mouth of night, mouth of Simeon Stylites
When the devil made his tongue into a bird's penis.
Take a handful of syllogisms, eat them.
Sit with the patience of gasoline,
Until after the last bomb has consumed its name;
And then, in a voice that is an hourglass,
A voice of the scissorings of time,
Bless the earth, bless the fire.

This You May Keep

A showering of branches,
Leaves in all their fits, their sultry shakes,
Like voices circling in a room,
Uninvited, but hovering, whirling,
An undulant map.

Surrender first your words:
On crisp stems, without pain or hope,
They defy all sense, all green.

Give up the future next:
There can be no waiting;
Even sloth is an urgent leafy crawl.

And the gaunt motorcyclist;
The old-fashioned mirror with no backing,
Only a tattered scar where your face is;
And the queen of dusty rooms,
The lady of hopes, give her up too.

This you may keep.
A smell of rain from the pavement,
This day of heat and mist.
And the leaves, their heavy silence;
Not even the hope of a way;
Only flesh in its looseness, its transactions with light,
Its whispering underfoot,
Its berries, some edible, some bitter.

Life Story

I

I speak, and don't want to lie.
How my past gives off a lean light;
Everywhere strangers inviting me, frightening me,
As if they were mysteries from God;
And I the only human being on earth.

I speak of sunlight on the roof-edge,
Listening to Mozart, a Vedic chant:
Twigs crackling in a fire;
While my wife shines in her mysterious rage.

II

If there is an Eden, it isn't past,
But coming: a beach in autumn;
A man trekking silently on the sand
While the sunlight rains down.
The stages of life pass by; the beach swelling
Its pale sprout, until it bursts
In showers of pain and light:
The fright of death, of growing old.

III

A boy with splayed ears,
A slack look on his face.
When I wake anxiously during the night,
A wall touches my eyelids
And I know he's on the other side,
Near a basement furnace,
A coal pile sparkling in the fire-glimmer.

I watch him push the cellar door
And feel his way downstairs,
While sweet summer air mingles
With musty coal, dark with dark.

His father and mother wheel among the galaxies;
He is the night's child. Not the dark's,
The child of space, of the low rumble
Shaking the air, like the god in the story
Slumbering fitfully under everything.

IV

The creak of an old floor;
A battered velvet couch, with her shape
Still hollowed in it;
A drunken swaying in the middle of the room,
Where our voices swerve and fall
Against a far wall.

Talking to her now,
Hearing her wake to a life she does not love;
Reading my life in her changed body,
While our daughter peers
Over the railing of her crib, frighteningly curious,
As if everything fit from beginning to end.
That's how the story begins.

The House

I

It has walls of the flat, breakable rock
Farmers still plough out of neighboring fields,
Roof beams of twisted oak,
Mortar of red clay, grooved deeply on the west
Where storms come in from the Atlantic
Over these once flooded hills.

It was built by a farmer's youngest son
Who took what was left, a few southward-
Tilted acres, chestnut woods, a pond.
This was wine country then;
The steep rocky slopes were good for that.
Along the hill crest, beside the old coach road,
Houses shepherded their vines.
Now, scrub oak and chestnut, lean spiked acacia.

The beautiful indifference of this land!
The brittle weeds in fields still half ploughed
From when he climbed into his bed, and never left it.
They say he was a short, likable man.
Who carved mystic runes on the doorpost,
And ploughed with a team of oxen,
Their horns sheathed in tin, harness
Of black oiled leather. I found the old yoke,
Dark with sweat, and polished it, hung it up,
To remind me that others had lived here
Before me; what I loved was their labor,
Elastic, hard as singing wire.

II

You don't build a stone house,
You coax it from the earth, like a bud
Perched on the mother-branch, and hugging it:
Walls a yard thick,
Windows narrow as *meurtrières*,

Roof tiles that gong when you strike them.
And a stone house doesn't change,
Like a farmer, thin and tanned
In his measureless old age.
Pacing his fields, his slowly ripening woods
Of oak and chestnut, death means nothing to him.

III
That first autumn I turned the garden with a pick and hoe,
Hammered an edge onto my scythe as my neighbor taught me;
I swam on the black earth, eating its glossy meat.
I heard no one, saw nothing.

My young wife listened to the radio
And grew thin. She became a silence.
Who could she talk to? Who could she dream of, and touch?
That fall the fireplace was her lover,
Her evenings licked into a phantom of fire.
At night, on the ridge,
She hooted at the oak fringe
Beyond the field. An owl's bell-like answer
Came, cautious and probing.
The moon pressed on the tiles of the house,
A ladder of clouds lowering the sky.

IV
That year something full of bitterness
And wild attention lived through me.
I watched the grape vines darken,
Their green fruit swelled, burst,
The rough cable of their trunks sagged to the ground.
Lizards ran in swift stabs over the gravel.
A walnut tree cast looping branches into the wind
That blew here when there were nothing
But forests, hermits, and devils tormenting them.

My wife and I slept in an oak bed, in the room
We had whitewashed, a single window,
Twisted irregular beams.
She hated the wildness, but even our bed
Where she took refuge, a square of soft clean linen,
Couldn't keep it from her.
Alone in that whiteness,
Listening to her deepest wish answering it angrily,
She became hard and pale.

V

When spring came, I planted dahlias
In a cleared patch near the house,
Gangly plants with heavy leaves
And thick bent heads that unclasped,
Red, purple, white.
They grew taller; stalks and flowers.
With their curved necks, they resembled
Unsmiling girls, their colors
Like a breath not fully breathed.

They were beautiful invalids, and I nursed them.
Crab grass and wild clover tried to choke them.
The ground hardened, the sun was heavy.
I carried pond water to them every evening,
Pulled the weeds up around their tough pink roots.
In the morning, I watched the flowers flare
And catch the early light.
By August, the tallest was as tall as I was.

How curiously human they looked,
How empty the house was.
My wife sat cross-legged on the oak bed.
Her door stood open to her enemy, the sun,
And her other enemy,
For by then I had become that.

VI

By now we couldn't see each other.
I was lonely, but couldn't say it;
We had become each other's negative,
Her body hardened by isolation,
And I, pleasureless, tough with need,
Wanting to be as motionless as the sun,
Predictable, walking with the heavy tread
Of the old men who had survived death,
And were now totems of brooding skin,
Leaning on two canes or
Straight as weeds on a hilltop.

How can I explain myself?
Here was refuge,
Here was the place I'd recognized,
Where I'd come to be saved from the fright of living;
These few acres cleared by people
I never knew, two stone rooms, floorless,
Cows breathing next to them,
The rafters creaking with the weight of harvest,
Wild fodder grass in the attic,
Tobacco hung in yellow sheathes
From the roof beams.
Time moved mutely in the leaves
Changing day by day,
In the yellowing lilacs, in the labored breath
Of the white sky blowing hot and long every day.

I can explain only myself,
But not the coldness that settled
Between us like a person,
The house thick with avoidance,
The lovelessness, the feeling that nothing
In the world existed but her expressionless face.
She was young, she had followed me here.
Now, after a year in this stone house,

A year of the rasping wind which blew
Before time began, and still makes its mockery
Of speech, which they heard in caves twenty thousand
Years ago, and witches heard in their dens
Of chestnut trees, and farmers on those stormy nights,
When the crops were at stake,
And I hear like a disorder in my mind,
There is nothing left between us
But our failure to understand.

The Question

Stone-blue winter;
The upswept brush of winter oak
Vibrates in the wind, expectant, bridelike.

Who am I?
An insect, startled, still sleeping
By the fire.

A bird clings to the telephone wire
Behind the house; an exultant questioning
Booms at its feet. When we die,
We hug the living to us as we never did;
We notice their creased skin, their quick eyes
That slide away, seeing more than they intended.

Who is that moving beside you,
So at ease, so colorless?
What can that dark flutter
Of his say to you, his voice thinned
To pass death's membrane?

Wasps

This morning I thumbed the spray-can,
And they stumbled from the rafters,
From the cheap rippled glass of the kitchen pane,
Until a striped carpet jerked over the tiles,
Or lay curled and still, like pebbles of bruised velvet.

When I cautiously churned a stick
Into their grey nest, papery, almost a mist,
The chaff of wing-wisps fluttered to the floor.
Now squads of ants tow them away.

A tractor's frayed howl rises from the valley.
Otherwise it is quiet, baked dust, marigolds.
Yet those heavy-bellied wasps stumbling over the tiles
Stay with me: their inaudible rage whines in my ear.
Listen to them in the pale stubble,
In the wild flowers, like small stings of color,
Poppy-red, cornflower blue.
My own breathing frightens me,
The precarious daylight hollowed by their knife-like wings.

Early Waking

Again the ashen light,
A tiny spider swinging on its pendulum thread
Against the pane.

Lately, I don't sleep much.
It's not anxiety, but a curious feeling
That I must pay attention, or death will gain on me.

A brightening across the valley,
Individual stalks of grass concentrate the light.
The red glossy leaves of the wild plum tree behind the house,
And the faded green nuggets of the young walnuts.
A cloud leans across the sky;
A faintly gusting wind in the oaks
And juniper, as if to say:
Nothing stops or begins, this whispering is all,
This tender faded light is all.

Parting the Sea

Fog hides the shallow ditch, no more
Than a grassy furrow, marking the edge of our land.
Oak trees and thorned acacia bend over it,
Like combers of a green sea.
The thinning out begins on this side,
Where there is barley, tobacco,
Green peas climbing on a spindly branch.
So much naming is not natural.
It must be cared for, thinned
And watered every day.
                              Listen!
The cruelty of trees, burst rivers
Of oak and fern, lap crazily around it.

To farm you need a sharp edge,
Something that doesn't know you're there;
You need to give up owning
This patch-sized farm on the earth's outer rim.

Remember the human body was trimmed
From something bigger and worse:
Identity sobs in the branches of trees,
Shouts from the stubble of the mown fields.
Either you have no enemies, or only enemies.

And Yet . . .

It's true, we carry the world inside us,
Always present like light.
And yet, this hilltop where the sun sits,
Heavy and red, every evening;
My house shuttered now, the gravel courtyard
Sprouting weeds; myself, woefully transient,
My suitcase packed, listening for
My neighbor who will take me to the train,
And the stillnesses mobbing past,
Strangely clamorous and thick.
It's true, I know. And yet, and yet!

The Other Ocean

1974

It was the whip-marks of the horned asp,
And the Beduin sucking his coffee
Through cracked fleshy lips;
It was his ceremonial kindness
In the month-long solitude of camel-watching,
While his animals bellowed over the plain
Like ghosts roaming in the star-glitter.
It was these scattered lives in a country without rain,
And the miniature within,
Crawling, hissing,
Its light almost solid, almost mineral.

The way back smelled of cinders,
Older, emptier than anything living;
A way of faces lost in the changes
Of light into dark, passing grief-wrinkled
Boulders, sand glaring red and grey.

It was a line of rust scrawled on the stillness,
As a sown darkness, and an expectation.

The Taking Away

The close-fitting sleepless night,
Everything still: the woodchuck in its hole
Under the rock pile, the apple tree outside my window.
In the aftermath of rain, a taking away:
Color, shape, sound, as if the darkness
Had flowed from my own eyes,
Dropping slow black flakes over the ground.

On nights like this, I think
Of a companion waiting in my armchair
For the first milk of dawn.
Not knowing his face, I say he looks like me.
I saw we fit one shadow, and that he once
Was grateful to the moon for following
Everywhere over the earth,
Even on that mineral night when everything
Human failed me, and I knew it would be years
Before I was whole enough to be a father,
Or a friend.

Now I lie awake in my New England brass bed,
Listening for lulls in the wind, when
The miles of birch and oak,
Patches of the fields between, breathe in;
And for a moment it is my breath,
My midsummer dark, veined with cold currents.
I am happy to lie in its shade,
To savor its fruit, and admire
Its icy grains sprouting down the night.

Eternity's Woods

I

I have come to this house
Of soft angular stone, wondering
How much must fall away before I have nothing.

Here is the raw path
That the Romans slashed across these hills,
And pilgrims trudged into crumbling rock;
Now it is an old scar, smelling of wild mint,
Rosemary, tiny wild orchids under the blackberry brambles.

The old farmer who built this place
On five acres of stiff red soil,
Good only for barley and a bitter wine,
Never saw a Jew in his life;
Yet I imagine him beside me,
His head tilted thoughtfully,
While a woodpecker jeers in the horse-chestnut tree.

II

I bought the house a dozen years ago.
For its calcareous stone, its oak beams so tough
They bend your nails. Even when there were vines,
And bitter grapes hung to the ground,
Only a poor farmer could have loved it.

Today his grandson, Jean, lives in the valley
Although he still comes up here when he can, to breathe freely
And tell me about the forest his grandfather knew;
The witches who cooked souls in open pots,
The quilted silence of the chestnut woods,
Where even brambles couldn't grow,
Only mushrooms that came and went, like odorous ghosts.

A hard red road scrapes the bones of the hill.
The parched field boils with cicadas;
A delirium of white scraps wobbling in the air,
Butterflies, the dance of life.

All my running has ended here:
The baked fragrant summer air,
The postman's yellow van coming to a halt,
The envelopes with their white chill of distance.

A shimmer of heat distorts eternity's woods,
And the butterflies wink over the field,
Half-wild, half-cruel,
Like the laughter of a solitary man.

III
There are times when you have nothing, are nothing:
A beach in cold October air
Breathing the space that held you;
Or a coal-dark basement, naked,
The night breeze garlanding your bare skin.

Now I have come to these clay-mortared rocks,
This walnut tree unraveling its shade
On the coarse gravel. Lying
On a manger ledge, in the bedroom, a stable once,
While iced fields of the Milky Way look on,
I wake in thick dark, unable to name my fright,
Until day drips, greys, and I come out into the leaf-gleams,
Alive in the bite of morning.

The End Circulates in the Wide Space of Summer

I
We hardly speak.
You have been here so long
You are like another leg or arm.
We trot across the ice,
Approach the book, and enter it.
You read the text,
I try to hear what you are saying.

The sky shivers,
A bird moves across it like a flexible blade.

So it began.

II
The end circulated in the wide space of summer,
With sawing of small insects, bubbles
Clustering in ponds.

I try to hear what you are telling me,
But the smile of an invisible cat consumes the sky;
That singsong call of young girls
Jumping rope is death's nursery rhyme.

III
Where in this endless room
Is the one who loves me,
The hissing of her silks?

We talk of God, his mica angels,
His book of living wormed in rock.
We have what lasts,
And the soft perishable mind, which doesn't.
We have the spacious word
Where nothing begins, and goes on beginning,
As long as we live.

Last Poems

Space Is the Wake of Time

Space is the wake of time,
Like the sound barrier expanding behind a plane.
Into the wreckage we hurry, over roads
That shimmer with the mirage.
Cars swim up in the pleated air,
Cities pass full of brown angles.
Their windows stare at us like cattle.
These are the cities Marco Polo left behind.
Now, baffling us with their cunning angles,
They stand as garlands of pure place,
Without any coming or going.
Not for them the disheartened wanderings of a lover,
Like exhausted blood returning to the heart,
Or the swallows gliding around a Tuscan tower,
Or the pigeons booming up out of a mottled well
Exhaling its breath of stale water.
Not for them the grey town
With a single car moving along the main street,
And a plump man in uniform waving
From the empty railroad platform,
As our bottomless window glides past
Full of pink houses, stacks of yellow hay,
Roads trickling uphill like weak desires.
And the creaking of an old clock;
The flies, like an empire without gravity;
The earthworms; the multiplication of living cells,
Which makes memory an entirely mysterious act,
An idea of stillness, extent without duration,
Identity borne on a disheveled wind,
Always different, always the same.

The Correspondence

The moon calls to it and it spills over the rocks,
Over the fine skin of the sand.
It is the lymph of the earth, slate-grey,
But rising into architectures of foam,
White beads, jewels that make you dream.
Thicker than air but malleable,
The graves we scoop in it heal and leave no trace;
The seeds we scatter on it never grow.
Its enormous eye stares upward, seeing
Nothing it will tell us. Its essence
Is movement, depth, cold, random shine,
And that peculiar swaying that lifts it,
As if with love, toward a dead star
Calling to it from afar.
Action from afar, resembling speech,
Or eyesight, is what we see in it;
And we see ourselves peering into our
Variable selves that are also thicker than air,
Full of darkness and random shine,
Staring upward and saying nothing of what they see,
Swaying with love, but changing,
Calm in one place while raging in another,
Splashing us with the wet of life,
While crushing and destroying somewhere else.

Piero

All that carnage: faces floating on the battle
Like torches of indifferent light,
A gold luminescence such as one sees in the large eyes
And the long muzzles of predators, unhurried,
Almost playful, in their killing skill.
These are faces of power, their color
A no color of pure thought, as if they were
Divided between their murderous acts
And the glimpse of something mute and pale
On which even death has no hold.
Spin out a story, cast it, and you will
Haul up river grass, roots, drownings,
All the sodden past that begins to shine
And harden in the thinning air:
Water-spirits,
The evil miniatures of fairytales,
The spirit of your childhood in the form
Of a salamander wriggling across last year's leaves
Beside a mountain
That cast a shadow; all that past, storyless,
But possessing the power to cast itself
Into unbidden combinations, like these fantasies
Of Piero della Francesca, the bowing women,
The men painted in soft pastels; or are the colors
Simply faded, as everything human softens and fades
Into a gift of presence?
The boy blows a trumpet as if he were exhaling
His youth, not his breath; the soldier grips
His sword in one fist, his arm reaching wide
As if to bare his soul; with his other
He holds a man by the hair. Time's furies
Roost on that out-stretched blade.
And the quiet!
Not even breathing is that quiet,
Not even thinking (constricting the capillaries,
And sending random electric impulses to the heart).
A leaf falling makes its own wind,

An earthworm chews the soil with a noise
That is silent only to our ears.
Everything living makes a noise:
An enormous, low, tangled, blind uproar,
Full of lulls,
Soft washes, purposeful threads of high persistent
Sound, forming a fabric, a trash heap,
A million trills, like the pillars of the mosque
Of hearts twanged by unknown winds,
As when the light staggers about, half-drunk,
And nothing is still but the midnight air
Of this apse where Piero worked by torchlight
Or sunlight, to tell his tale of the tree of life
Becoming fire, dream, a cross, a bridge over nothing.
And these faces, little vacuums,
That say there is more here than what we see,
More than noise, dancing, more than light
And these faded gentle colors;
More than the gift of presence.

Skywriting

White furrow on the sky for the seed that will not grow,
The laborious skywriting, like a child
Tracing his name in stabbing lines of letters:
Graffiti, pyramid, stone cross, footprint, haystack;
Or the farmer wielding the shoulder-bone of an ox,
Who first shoveled up the earth and planted
Barley, half-wild wheat; who let fall the seed
Of his cock, and sucked the black wound
Where the earth bled food. And the shell-heaps;
The fifty-ton stones turned on end;
The mounds to keep the dead from getting loose:
All those acts to keep life from getting out of hand,
The dead shells of deeds forming another kind of life.
The 120-foot-high earthen nipple of Silsbery
Took a hundred years to erect out of chalk blocks,
Rubble, and a fine skin of earth.
What a job for a handful of shepherds
Who also ploughed the soil in their season:
A laborious outcry, meaning here! Or a curse.
Curse the intractable earth, death, blindness, rotten teeth,
Arthritis, dead babies; curse winter, curse summer!
Can you hear me, heaven? Am I making enough noise
For you? Suck on this teat of dust and rock.
I'm dying down here, and I want you to hear
The sound of it. It is called scream in the night,
It is called earth tit and Stone Henge,
It is called language,
It is called the sleeplessness of the gods.

The Thick World

You have come this far into the thick air,
And you are alone, breaking thickness.
It's the damnedest thing:
The chill, the fishy light,
Those armies of unnamed swimmers
Lifting off, hovering; they're all here.
The redhead moaning in his Paris attic
At the crystallography in his mind;
The sallow wife of a sallow friend,
Disclosing secrets of pain in her motionless voice.
And you, father, riding your bicycle
On the brown scimitar of the shore
That leads to heaven, father I longed for
In the mad hopelessness of my young manhood,
What are you doing here in the place
Where breath comes hard?
"Son," he spoke thickly, "I've been
Waiting for years to tell you: I want to take back
The life you stole from me, the one
I never lived because I gave it to you,
You naughty boy. Why didn't you leave
Some for me? You didn't have to take it all."
"What do you mean, father?
All I did was cringe whenever you swung
Your heavy arm. All I did
Was slip into your hidden mind and see
The fallow poems, and try to write
A few of them, and try to be happy . . . fat chance."
There on the green floor
Is my mother sweeping thickness.
It is the thick world, the place of lunar dancing.
"Why aren't you dancing, mother?
Why are you wearing away the darkness
With your broom? You are so busy,
It must be polished and clean down there
By now. Can you see your reflection
On the perfect floor? Your thinning
Hair, your anxious hands, hardly a trace
Left of the slender girl who looked on

With fright, and maybe a little love,
At the thing you had given birth to,
Hairless and pink, weeping with helpless rage,
But packed with future, like an empty mirror,
On a night sky littered with stars."
Oh, the living down there!
Oh, the green light where appetites rant,
A little berserk, nipping playfully at you
Until they tug loose small bitefuls
And wag off in thick air. Secret appetites,
Huge dark one with rows of teeth;
Appetites that sing and appetites that whisper;
Blind appetites, and far-seeing ones
That cast their glance beyond the horizon.
Why is it so thin up here?
Why do we reach for each other with hands
Cramped by thickness? If it weren't for our pain,
We might fly up like little parachutes,
Until the world was a shaved face,
And the clouds sang to us of light
With no sun, sweetness with no honey.
In the crooked shade of a pine tree
A man speaks softly,
And his words rumble, full of whimsy.
"Are you thirsty?" he sings.
"This clay pot gushes from a thousand holes.
Crocodiles breed in it; flowers riot in it.
Grab hold of it, and your lips will taste
The generations of the trees,
The wildness of extinguished stars.
Is that what you want?" he sings.
"The gushing pot, or this," and he held
Out to me a flower.
I could feel it opening inside me.
In the cup of the flower I saw him,
Rumbling and wheezing. Again the flower
Opened, again I saw him. Flower
Within flower, singer within singer.
All the dust of creation in the flower.

Poem

Why can't anything stay still?
Even the earth rolls through space like a bruised plum,
And trees work secretly in the ground
Like old men with treacherous toes.
The air shifts and settles further on,
Flutters up like a wild heart, and bursts,
Until it fidgets into life again, like a horse's
Skin quivering at the touch of those ugly flies
That buzz heavily and then, with a random
Sting of truly intractable pain,
Stab through the finely haired membrane.
Why can't anything stay still?
That was Pascal's question, God
As idea of stillness, in a small room;
His nights filled with "Fire, fire, fire,"
Nights that didn't drive him into the streets
Until a first café switched on its lights,
And he went in, his face stiff,
A slab of flesh,
His eyes stinging, and ordered a big cup of *café au lait*.
Not that sort of night!
But nights of a thousand years, mysteriously inward
And paralyzed, lucid, bitter; nights of the food
That never cloys and the light that shines wildly
As on the day the animals received their names
And swam and ran in terror, stung by a new sort of clarity.

Poem

The farmers are pumping water from the river,
Pumping shadows. They are hauling up night
And spraying it over the river fields.
Wheels of dusk revolve over the tobacco sprouts
And the buddings of corn;
The poplars are rooted in it; the stone church
Catches the last light as it goes by, and holds on.
The green turrets of the *platanes* loom blue,
And the barley patches, blinding yellow, dry as hope;
The walnut tree disheveled and solitary in a vast field,
And the river like a black nerve amid all these colors;
The pump stuttering its night song
Of water, drowsing, waiting for the light
To disappear from the tilted church,
From the tops of the poplars
Weaving their conga line up the valley.
                                        The farmer
Takes off his wooden shoes and claps them together
With a snap heard a mile away, lumbering
Over the broad oak boards, and lets himself into bed.
On the hillside an owl gongs its hollow note.
Water wheels softly over the vanished field;
The pump, having gorged the world with night,
Isn't satisfied. It stutters, pulses,
Now it is boring into the sleep-world
Looking for the night-bird, Orpheus,
Who played songs of light and time,
The poppies, hawthorne,
Queen Anne's lace, cornflowers
And wild blackberry.
But the king of the dead scoffed
And the poet plucked harsh notes, sudden downpours.
Lovers stuck together with sweat,
As if time had melted, and the light slanting
Through the window, shifting and grey,
As clouds tumble past, were the light of heaven.
The king of the dead remembered a dream:
A girl crowned with flowers
That wilted as she descended,

Yellow, red and pink. As she came toward him,
She too became old; her hands were thin and hard.
She said nothing, but he saw the world of light
Where everything lived for a while, and then died.
Unbelievable! A disorder of living and dead,
Rich and strongly smelling. The nose lived there,
And the mouth, wild with the taste of air and rain,
Of the ocean, fish and animals. It was too much!
Calling out his heat to the empty woods,
The king of the dead fell in love with the productions
Of time. Like a shimmer of droplets slipping
Between gusts of wind, they came: time's litter,
The residue of life.
The king of the dead held his hand out,
Tasted it, and a wildness possessed him.
But the rain became dust,
Falling into the far corners, softening, a silent snow,
Thick, unvarying, a lid on a death.
And now he saw the lifefall,
He saw a chain of lights climbing and descending;
As the poet plucked his buzzed notes,
Like hornets in the cave of the dead,
The stone girl became flesh again,
And he saw an ascending rain.
It was the song: tough handfuls of notes,
And the high keen voice, not beautiful,
An ugly voice that seemed to climb out of a pit,
Full of stinks and grindings, its slap
Of wet leather and old ill-fitting pistons,
Chugging out of the heart beyond the poplars,
Where the field curves down to the river,
And the black leavings of day,
The corn, the domed sproutings of tobacco,
Expand in the life-flood,
Wheeling, falling upon them in a spray
That the king of the dead will never know,
Although he dreams of it in delicious nightmares,
Feeds on it, and watches the long litter
Of love descending.

Poem

I don't know if I can bear this suddenly
Speeded-up time. I pull the blinds
And it is morning: white flowers gleam
Under the linden leaves; the cathedral's red dome
Dwarfs the timid skyline across the river.
A town like any other: cars grinding
Over the cobbles, the perishable mosaic of fruits
And vegetables in front of small stores.
The dead look on indifferently from their green horses,
From their pedestals, where they receive the homage of pigeons.
There are no old men, only brown, mocking boys
And girls dancing out of their clothes.
The old men loiter, silent and transfigured,
In museums, nursing their small immortalities.
Can you smell it? The car fumes, coffee, breath,
Old leather, urine, a young woman's perfume.
It smells of youth, death, sleepless nights;
It never looks up, doesn't see
The blank enduring looks of the statues;
And yet it is a kind of poem.
But now I'm thinking of those green men
Concentrated in their single, undistracted movement,
Their heads pulled belligerently back
While they tug on the reins of a bronze horse,
Their eyes like termites boring holes in nothing,
Because they have hit on the one gesture
That will never fail of completion,
Their whole perishable selves squeezed into
A green eroded look that chuckles at the stupidities
Of springtime and young girls, from their own springtime
Of ominous, wretched, sour verdure.
Oh, the egotists, the zany gods commemorating
One or another of the lies men tell
To garnish their forgettable lives: the legends,
Bibles, enormous whisper rising like a cloud of bees,
A shimmer of golden motes,
And their honey! Fluid as water, transparent, sweet,
So that anyone who tastes it forgets father and mother,

Lover, children, money, cancer, failed hopes.
Oh, the cunning among stones, turning the fear of life into the
    love of life.
The statues, all to their monomaniacal greenness,
Enjoy the joke, although they don't laugh,
Or even smile; while the girls gather their black hair into a bun,
And the boys call out mysterious passwords of blood and sperm
And a sweet smell comes from the fruit stands, where cherries,
Apricots, peaches, plums soften and sag;
A cloying liquid wets the tilted boxes, darkening the sidewalk.
Soon it will be evening.

Poem

To know it all deeply, to know every detail,
To see it pressing from the motionless leaves,
And the blue mist which, even in summer,
Assembles over the tilted fields
And the dark turmoil of the oak woods
As a breath, a negligent exhaling,
From the night just past.
To see it on the grey lid of the cistern,
Half overgrown with thorns and barbed weeds;
In the avuncular walnut trees
With their green eggs and their lanky
Branches almost sweeping the ground;
In the bleached rug of barley,
Past ripe now, and stiff as straw,
Waiting for my neighbor, Jean-Claude, to reap it
In a clatter of loose bolts and half-greased cogs,
His red scratched tractor
Tilting over the hard ruts of old plantings,
Shaking his spine, while he waves over and smiles
His muscular, fast-talking smile; the smile
Of the son of a fast-talking father,
Who used to tell stories all day and yell
Like a teapot, a small, thin, immaterial man,
Who could take a truck apart with a screwdriver
And put it back again; who was out on his tractor
The day after a heart attack, bitching and wheezing
With his thin grim laugh, which couldn't believe
A man was made to lie down except when he was dead,
Or maybe for a few fitful hours when the sun
Had the bad grace to hide behind the earth,
And there wasn't enough light to fix a machine,
Milk a cow or zoom up the vein of bleached rock
We call a road, to some patch of soil studded
With rocks, and plough, or rip up stumps;
Or even, when a faint blue unzipped
Over the eastern trees, to slip into his famous
Chestnut woods with a wicker basket and a short knife
And, late in summer, after the mid-August storms,

Poke about for those brown, perfect domes
With milky meat and fat stems bulging like barrels;
They call them *bolets, cèpes,* or simply *champignons,*
As if every other kind of earth-smelling knob,
The red or white ones, the black death-trumpets,
The humorous flesh-orange twists called *chanterelles,*
Were simply God's litter, but not the true meaty
Smoky steak-thick mushroom. The old man was a terror
And a marvel. They all shook when he was around;
And Jean-Claude, a big-shouldered boy,
Knew every modulation of his anger,
Every impatience, every unstoppable shake
Of his thin arms, his over-alive face,
And merely would stand there. Until one day his father
Was killed. A circular saw exploded and he breathed
Fire into his lungs. His body was a pincushion
Of slivers. He wasn't so old, not even sixty.
He was planning to tear around the countryside forever,
But the fire got him. His lungs fell apart
And, strangely fat with cooked skin and fever,
His small busy eyes knowing everything, he said:
"Ça y'est, cette fois."
                                This is it, I know it.
To know it all deeply; to have it press up
Like earth-blood out of the crooked old peach tree
In front of the house, propped up on sticks,
But nursing its peaches year after year
Until it seems to hunch lower and want to lie down,
And the peaches swell with long-cooked sweetness,
Orange, yellow and pink.
To know the knobby dried-out grass
And the greying green of late summer
Like a happiness on the earth, a ripening
Into heat and dryness, plums, chestnuts, leeks,
Into tobacco and walnuts,
And the evil-smelling pigs resembling trapped men
In their rooted-up squares of yard
Full of stumps and furrows and dead trees,

All to make it happy, that creature of fat and flesh
And delicious blood, every ounce of whom
Will be cut up, bled off, ground up,
Until only a few bones will end up feeding the dogs.
Its guts stuffed full of cooked blood
Will hang in the attic; its hams, packed
In a chest of salt, will stew all winter;
Its flesh, salted and ground with juice of truffle,
Will cook in jars and be saved.
To know every inch of it; every wind sliding
From the west full of wet ocean air;
Every pinched odor of the paper mill ten miles north:
The distant grumble of the machines
That augur of good weather, north weather.
And every variety of silence, the vocabulary
Of it not in our language: the cicadas on hot afternoons,
Pine worms creaking in the rafters,
The leanings of white barley, and the hum
Of small winds on the ear, almost an internal sound,
A blood sound. The silence before
The dawn colors begin and the blue silence of the last light
With a couple of large stars;
Layerings of it, full of speech
And smells, and of all except the human voice.
To know it year after year: to know the slide
Into winter, the last feeble pushings of fodder grass
Not worth harvesting, unless you turn the cows loose in it,
And watch the brown turds form like flowers
On the yellow ground.
The hunters stumbling past apologetically;
The hollow roar of their shotguns;
A couple of deer bounding across my field one morning,
Their hooves making a faint thunder;
And behind them the baying of the dogs,
A crew of mongrels with pink, daffy tongues.
Long afterward the hunters arrive, their guns slung under their arms,
More interested in the bottle in their bag,
In the chilly light, and the indolent friendly day,

Than in the deer who are probably over the next hill
By now, trembling knee-deep in leaves,
While the dogs, more spoiled pets
Than hunting dogs anyway, chase their tails
And splash in a pond.
To know so much; to take these five acres
Of fruit trees, acacia and chestnut;
The puny fields, the house built with flat stones
Ploughed out of the ground and cemented with
Red clay, its roof of crooked oak beams
And tiles so old they sing in the rain;
To spy the cretaceous fossil shells that speak
Of ancient seas, and the shining flints
That speak of men, and know I am here,
And have been here; that time has spread its wares;
That every stone has its story,
Every wind speaks its mind, and there is
A birth-giving, a bringing-forth of days
That is not time, but space; memory;
The irrecoverable home.

About the Author

A respected literary critic and author of books in philosophy and biography, Paul Zweig wrote three other volumes of poetry, *Against Emptiness, The Dark Side of the Earth,* and *Eternity's Woods* (Wesleyan 1985). His 1984 study *Walt Whitman: The Making of the Poet* was nominated for a National Book Critics Circle award.

Born on Bastille Day in 1935 in Brooklyn, New York, Zweig felt his "deepest sense of place" in France, where he lived part of each year in the Dordogne. A graduate of Columbia University (B.A. 1956, M.A. 1958), he received a doctorate in comparative literature from the Sorbonne, University of Paris, in 1963. He was professor of comparative literature at Queens College and divided his time between France and New York. He died in Paris in August 1984.

About the Editor

C. K. Williams is the author, most recently, of *Poems 1963–1983.* His book *Flesh and Blood* won the National Book Critics Circle award for 1987. He is professor of English at George Mason University in Fairfax, Virginia.

About the Book

This book was composed on the Mergenthaler 202 in Galliard, a contemporary rendering of a classic typeface prepared for Mergenthaler in 1978 by the British type designer Matthew Carter. The book was composed by Marathon Typography Service of Durham, North Carolina, and designed and produced by Kachergis Book Design of Pittsboro, North Carolina.